Getting Started
with Real Estate Marketing

Getting Started with Real Estate Marketing

KEVIN REID SHIRLEY

About the Author

KEVIN REID SHIRLEY is a real estate professional with almost twenty-five years of experience. He is an Associate Broker with Long & Foster Real Estate in Washington, DC. He is an Accredited Staging Professional and Graduate, REALTOR Institute. He graduated from the University of Mary Washington with a Bachelor of Arts Degree in Classical Civilization and Art History. He speaks real estate fluently!

Table of Contents

Introduction

Marketing for real estate agents may have been simple, years ago, but times have changed. There's more competition now, and you do not know if you can stay productive in a market in which agents are closing shop daily. You have to think outside the box.

Marketing strategies that used to work no longer do because today, those promotion techniques are outdated. To thrive, you must innovate and demonstrate you're a confident business.

You may be tempted to let basic business principles slide, though it is essential to hold on to these. You must look for the right answers in the correct places. But do not keep your old marketing techniques rather, throw them out. Assess your current practices with a critical state of mind, aiming to find mistakes in your methods and discover what's not working. You're certain to see numerous things which aren't working. Your approach requires honing current practices and trying new ones to overtake others in the real estate sector.

First, write a list, summarizing areas in which your business is better compared to others. Then, look for a niche that isn't competitive and apply those suggestions in this niche. This is how marketing for real estate agents succeeds.

Applying new marketing ideas is easier said than done but will prove essential. Consider a daring branding change, like modifying your business colors and a new logo. If huge businesses like Microsoft can change rapidly and boldly, there's no reason why you cannot too.

Look at what others are doing, and put together a summary of their good ideas. They may be performing some things well, other things less so. Learn from their errors to improve your own strategy.

In this guide, you will learn the secret techniques most real estate agents either don't know or don't apply, that will attract new buyers and sellers every month, by using effective marketing methods.

I hope it helps.

A MARKETING FACELIFT

In recent years, the real estate marketing landscape has changed considerably. What used to be relatively effortless is now a challenge. Real estate has therefore become a highly competitive space. Real estate agents must deal with the fact that earlier marketing methods are behind the times and no longer do the job.

The vast majority of real estate is promoted with an actual estate agent behind it because the majority of property owners do not have the time to manage a submission or the flow of inquiries or may not even understand the process.

Nowadays, one of the primary aspects of any real estate agent marketing plan is putting information online. This ensures not just being seen by many prospects but also provides data like how many visitors have come to your website and looked at individual listings, at any time of the day. Online listings also enable you to observe the return on investment (ROI) on your marketing, allowing you to see which visitors converted into clients.

WHAT DO CLIENTS WANT?

Online, prospective clients use search criteria to filter their results by far more than just location and value.

In print, often you'll find much more than just a couple of listings from real estate agents in the newspaper. Many feature regular pullout sections vital marketing when done properly.

In real life, giving out business cards is handy; spreading the word about your brand locally can lodge in the mind.

This is difficult to do in a crowded market, however. These strategies are old and in this real estate crisis, they're losing effectiveness fast.

You must think outside the box and take advantage of confirmed marketing methods. This might include using your website to provide other critical info that prospective clients can make use of.

For instance, you can offer a free report on the state of your market, you can provide a report advising how to get the best value for a home, or maybe a report for customers on how to get the house of their dreams at a reduced price.

You must represent yourself as the specialist in the area. You must specialize somehow to stand out from your peers.

When you're dedicated to offering sellers and buyers of real estate whatever they require, you are going to be more effective. Among the best marketing strategies is simply to be recognized as dependable to the industry.

People looking to purchase real estate usually wish to be walked through the task so it's as easy as possible. Using several marketing techniques, therefore, will be the best method to ensure you receive all the clients you can deal with.

To achieve success, you need to be able to hold on to the fundamental aspects of your small business in your marketing. Do not remain too attached to the particulars because they aren't helpful. If you're searching for new solutions, you have to have a flair for inventing effective formulas. You'll probably find many areas of the formula which don't do the job any more. Thus, you must be willing to reinvent your strategy and open yourself to brand new ideas. Keep in mind a great idea can come from anywhere and even the janitor may think of an excellent idea if you're ready to accept it.

When coming up with a marketing tactic, you must consider how to be distinct from your competitors. You have to think of something nobody is doing.

It can help if you identify a market to target that is rewarding but not so highly competitive. Additionally, it can help if you conceive a new brand. This can be quite a task but if effective, you can breathe new life in your old image.

Consider the example of Microsoft's search engine Bing. Microsoft reinvented how it thought about search and breathed new life into an old idea, and it caught on.

Learn from your competitors' errors and have the nerve to try out new things. Experimentation typically results in something you never considered.

The largest obstacle real estate agents are going to encounter is how to boost the amount of clients they have, finding consumers who are genuinely interested and searching for a home to live in.

Continue reading to learn helpful approaches to get more customers without spending massive time in developing your business.

Strategy 1
Email Marketing

Email marketing has been around in the real estate industry for some time and is a good option compared to regular offline marketing. It was crucial to real estate firms after the subprime crisis, which almost destroyed the real estate industry, when serious cutbacks were made to operating expenditures.

With the present surge of demand for real estate, in line with a recovering economy, there's a need to retain the advantage of online marketing, so a real estate agent will need to guarantee communications from mail delivery to converting the recipient.

This is a challenging business, as encryption programs continue to be costly, although this appears to be changing. Nevertheless, the strategies of email marketers must adapt to the increasing practice of email encryption. Encryption is essentially a scrambling technique which sends a passkey along with a contact message. To anybody else who would like to snoop in on the information, the email would simply be a scrambled display of junk characters. But when the email gets to the intended recipient, they have the passkey to unscramble the email and read it. The advantage of encryption is to generally enhance safe interaction from one end to the other.

Email marketing may not secure a line of interaction since you can't expect all your clients to purchase encryption software; thus, the line of securing communications will be just between servers.

This is great from a company standpoint since you don't want your special offers and interactions with a lead to go out into the marketplace, for your competitors to get a hold of them. Note that encryption programs won't make you immune to a spam filter. Once again, this is due to the server-protected communication link, which can't be given to a recipient. But theoretically, if your recipient does have encryption software, then no spam filter could block the mail.

An essential element of encryption, when offering it with your clients, is the fact it commercially separates you from spammers and protects your customers from spammers. This is simply because spammers are likely to snoop around on the web and with the assistance of hackers, go after unsecured communications, parse email messages for mail addresses, and next begin spamming your buyers.

The responsibility will then fall upon you for not securing communications and ensuring your customers' privacy. Not protecting your recipients' privacy is something which could get you into legal trouble. Hence, you have to purchase encryption to perform email marketing.

Strategy 2
Using Real Estate Directories

Whenever you mention directories, people would historically think of the Yellow Pages or White Pages. To the new world of technology and the web, people are switching to online directories.

If you are searching for a product or service which is regional or local, I cannot think of something more local than real estate. An Internet directory is a fantastic option when you are searching for an agent to help you purchase or sell.

WHAT IS A REAL ESTATE DIRECTORY?

A real estate directory is a set of pages categorized to make things simpler to find. The information may be organized according to region, agent, property type, specialty of the agent, etc.

You will find directories which concentrate on properties on the market, while others supply a list of local agents. You can find listings for home inspectors, contractors, appraisers, and just about anything to do with real estate.

WHY USE A REAL ESTATE DIRECTORY?

Approximately 80% of homebuyers start looking for a house on the Internet. It's essential to have not just a user-friendly site but also a solid web presence.

Numerous agents have their own sites but also publish listings to websites as HomeGain, REALTOR.com, and many others. Apart from marketing your listings, listing your website in directories is a great method to help you generate targeted visitors to your site.

However, since these directories have links to and from a lot of relevant sites, it is more important to rank higher in the search results of sites like Google than any single REALTOR website.

If you publish your site to a real estate directory, you are using the authority of and page ranking of the directory to bring visitors to your site. One more reason to list your site on a directory is that buyers and sellers also browse these web directories for local agents.

Strategy 3
Internet Marketing

As a real estate professional, you no doubt understand the real estate market is in as generously reported a slump.

It is harder to qualify for home loans now. If you're attempting to find a far better method to put your inventory of homes on the market, remember that online marketing creates views.

Classic real estate marketing has incorporated direct mail, community newspaper ads, and good old fashioned cold calling on the phone. These time-tested marketing techniques work fine in a bull market but how can you discover new clients in a bear market? You need a strategy to draw clients from outside the conventional marketing sectors.

Drawing consumers from outside the nearby area could be the only method for a real estate professional to move their inventory of homes. Arbitrary mailouts are ineffective as are cold calls to out-of-region individuals.

The web offers the perfect medium to make your inventory of houses available to out-of-region clients. It allows potential homeowners to see readily available listings from the convenience of their own home. The listings of any REALTOR may be published on the web for a low price.

Marketing a property on the web will provide extra listings to the agency from sellers who want to spread the publicity of their home to buyer, leading to a quicker purchase and happier clients.

The existing MLS listing form can be reproduced on a PC or even a simplified form may be produced. Together with the listing, detailed pictures of the house can be incorporated.

A far more upscale technique for enabling potential customers to see the house is providing a video clip. The video may be incorporated into the online listing in a WAV format. Windows Media Player and other media players can view this easily. The addition of a video walk-through of the interior and exterior of the house gives a potential client the ability to walk through the house without setting foot in it.

The addition of a description, the MLS listing, pictures and a video of the property reduce the short list of homes the buyer must go visit. Online marketing thus expands the client base, improving the agent's bottom line. Sellers find online marketing appealing since it raises the exposure of the property to more customers. This can lead to even more listings for the agency.

Online marketing brings in more prospective clients by growing your base of free clients.

The prospect's ability to see your listings at home enables them to figure out what residence interests them and saves the agent time, reducing the number of live tours given to prospects. Internet marketing therefore saves the agency cash and offers far more profit to each sale.

Strategy 4
Property Video Marketing

Estate agents have advertised to clients in the same conventional way for a while, now. Tiny pictures in the property section of papers and specialized magazines, two or perhaps three pictures on a business site, and displays in the business's windows.

However, real estate agents have embraced the strength of video to promote residential and commercial property to a worldwide market. With 80% of customers starting their property search online, it is a logical step to take.

Property videos can be seen by prospective customers wherever they are. Rather than the typical two or three photographs, a slide show video can incorporate 20-30 images and sellers with a larger budget can have their property professionally filmed.

This enables the customer to enjoy a virtual tour of the property and surrounding area like they were there, from the convenience of their home.

Banners and titles can integrate a lot more info regarding the property, including music, narration, or voiceover and a professional presenter can add that additional master touch to promote the property.

Property videos are vital, and save the estate agent, property owner, and customer time and money from pointless viewings. They can be embedded upon the estate agent website or even uploaded to YouTube or Vimeo. A URL link may be emailed to consumers.

So picture a purchaser in New York, Dubai, or Hong Kong. They can look at a selection of property videos from their desktop or even a cellphone, seeing a fuller picture of the listing and therefore being ready to purchase a new house before they even come to town.

Strategy 5
Mobile Marketing

With the advancements of mobile marketing, real estate agents must be reaping the benefits. Text message marketing gives agents, landlords, and mortgage brokers unparalleled instant access to clients. Conventional marketing techniques including email, direct mail, and print are quickly becoming the resources of yesterday. Nowadays, it's all about mobile.

Given the declined state of the real estate market and the battles that many agents are facing, affordable and powerful marketing methods will be the answer. Mobile media is certainly a vital part of this.

WAYS TO USE MOBILE MARKETING

People go nuts when they lose sight of their mobile phones even for a few seconds, as if our lives depend on it. Admit it! The second you have a spare minute, the first thing you do is reach out for it to check Twitter, Facebook updates, messages, replies, emails, or likes. You look for the most up-to-date news happening internationally and locally, the stock market, the weather, your calendar, and just about anything and everything.

Let's face it, a contemporary lifestyle is focused around mobile. Mobile phones are no longer limited to easy voice communication. We've turned into information interaction via MMS and SMS. Furthermore, smartphones are not simply for basic correspondence or keeping in touch with friends and loved ones. Mobile communication is now important for business.

Out of 5.3 billion mobile users worldwide, more than 300 million are in the USA. Imagine promoting your services as a real estate agent in America and making your listings easily available to all of these individuals, to look at any time of the day. Mobile marketing makes it possible and it is a key method for growing your business.

REAL-TIME NOTIFICATION

If you use SMS marketing, you'll assign a brief code to each property and a short contact number for business use. Customers can use this number to make a property inquiry by text.

You'll then get real-time notification that provides you with the opportunity to get in touch with the buyer instantly.

A consumer might send an inquiry to your short number to receive details of the property and your contact details by text. You just assign various codes to each property in the listing to be delivered to one central number.

A good example is for a prospect to text the code â€œA90210â€ to the number 2211 to get info on House A in Beverly Hills. Upon sending that code, the client will get a quick response with the property details, as well as your contact number, site, and email. You might include in your reply pictures, links or video clips for them to see the property without walking into it. Mobile streaming saves both the client and you a large amount of time.

With mobile marketing, you don't have to invest a lot of cash or much. At a tiny proportion of the cost of a billboard, print, radio, or

TV, mobile marketing can effortlessly be set up to provide ready access to property info and contact details.

Running a business by remaining true to tradition won't help you any longer. Change is a necessity. To benefit, you must move with the times. We're living in the mobile revolution, and mobile marketing is the most effective option.

Mobile marketing is by far the most life-changing business method we've observed in the past decade. Not only does it set you apart from the competition, but customers like this particular marketing method.

Business cards in newspapers are out, while text messages are in. For a substitute of giving out business cards, you can send out your information to clients in a text format. It's an easy method to create a database of leads that's permission based.

Agents can keep in better keep in contact with prospective clients by texting info in real time to tell them about new property listings. This will speed up the sales process along with clients feeling especially well catered for. This particular marketing type can boost follow-ups on prospective leads, and enhance the customer experience.

Strategy 6
Social Media

Social networking is a driving force for real estate agents and their online marketing efforts. Agents who have neglected the social marketing bandwagon have to adapt their mindset or risk being left in the dust by local competitors who are extremely visible online.

Establishing a powerful social media presence allows agents to successfully promote themselves and their listings through a wide range of (free) community channels, all while creating an identifiable brand image that's well recognized.

There are two social Internet marketing websites which real estate agents must think about joining to further their social networking and brand recognition.

FACEBOOK

Facebook is the largest social networking site on the planet, making it difficult not to completely focus a little time and effort into. Creating a Facebook page must be on your social Internet marketing to-do list. Here are some vital strategies for Facebook marketing:

Post useful, valuable content. Users do not read things which do not interest them. They do not care about whom you are having lunch with or where you are having your pedicure. They want useful information regarding the real estate industry, updates on your listings, when/where you are showing houses, and links to great content that's going to interest them.

Engage people to leave comments and reply to them in kind if they do. That is the reason it is called social networking. It connects you with other people online.

Encourage friends to like and share the company page. It is going to help you get more supporters and increase the brand visibility across people's newsfeeds.

Facebook advertisements can help your real estate brand gain more visibility in the local market, and you have exceptional demographic targeting abilities.

LINKEDIN

LinkedIn is a remarkably effective social networking platform for real estate agents due to its focus on professional networking. LinkedIn provides a special platform to network along with other real estate agents, through real estate groups who can refer listings in areas they don't cover.

Additionally, it provides the capability to connect with clients and show up in their LinkedIn newsfeed. You can connect with various businesses and co-workers in any nearby area, and acquire far more publicity for your agency. Build credibility as a reliable resource in the market by posting important content and interacting with various other users.

Strategy 7
Copywriting

Whenever we speak about copywriting for real estate agents, it pertains not just to sales letters you could be sending to your mailing list but to classified advertisements, postcards, your site, business cards, and any place where you use text to market your services. Copywriting boils down to composing excellent product sales pitches.

As an agent, you will need sound, interesting, eye-opening copywriting, present throughout your marketing material. It may sound extreme, but experiment with hiring a copywriter to boost your sales power in every message you communicate.

The first thing you need is to know the market. That can determine how you create, what words you use, and the approach you integrate in the copywriting. Primarily, you are writing to customers of real estate, but even that can be segmented into home sellers, first time buyers, VA customers, etc.

Every segment is going to differ in demographic and therefore react to a slightly different message. For instance, first time buyers are generally a little younger and respond differently to the seller of a $5 million home.

You will ideally target each of the categories separately. But do not go overboard with this since the market place may be a geographic area and not always possible to split into various demographics. Remember, your prospects are customers, rather than exclusively business professionals, which means you can create a personable, conversational tone for the most part. Let the personality shine through the copywriting!

The next thing you must accomplish is knowing the brand. You will need to integrate the brand into the copywriting. If your brand is about elegance, for instance, you will want the writing to reflect that. If your brand is all about being young and hip, you must create that. Either way, you must distinguish yourself from other agents through your copywriting.

Thirdly, work out what idea you are attempting to convey and how to word that message. This is the essence of copywriting. Bear in mind, you are targeting what the prospect is thinking, being, wanting. Do not speak to them about yourself specifically, or simply how good you are. They wish to be engaged with, not talked to. Focus on their feelings. Figure out what they need and write in such a manner to grab them and speak to their heart.

Place yourself in their shoes at all times. In creating any content, clear your mind and pretend you're the prospect. Read the piece and consider whether it spoke to you, and whether it relates for them, on an emotional and personal level.

Regarding the technical aspects of writing a sales message, there are three primary parts (there are a great deal more but these are the core ones) in nearly every marketing message, whether a business card, email or text ads:

1) Headline

2) Benefits

3) Call to action

Headlines are essential but overlooked by a lot of people. Everybody says "Do not judge a book by the cover," though we all do. And that is precisely what a title is: a cover. For instance, imagine you visit Barnes & Noble and look in the baking section for a guide on Thai Stir Fry. You are flipping through these books, reading through the titles (headlines) and possibly reading more or just placing each book back. You are creating a split-second decision to continue or quit, depending on the name (yes, the pictures come into play, but that is another topic). If the name seems great, you will generally pick up the book and read the back. If the name stinks, you will not think twice and you will move on to the next book.

Yet another example is looking at the job advertisements on Craig's List. All you get is a title and you've to click it to find out about the particular task or product. Do you sit there and click on every headline? No. You search through the headlines and click on the interesting ones. So in your own copywriting, make them wish to find out what will happen next.

Benefits. You may have read before: "Emphasize the advantages, not the features," or maybe "Features tell but advantages sell." This distinction must be recognized in your own sales copy.

A feature will be "Five bedrooms." An advantage will be "Five roomy bedrooms, so the children are not yelling at one another at bedtime." The feature simply states what it is. The advantage points out just what it does for the prospect; in this instance, it relieves them of screaming, fighting children.

A benefit does something for somebody. Generally, there might be an "oversized dining room" but that will not catch anyone's interest until you explain what that oversized dining room is going to do allow the family to have dinner together and create long-lasting memories at Thanksgiving.

You must create advantages which hit your prospects rather than tell them details that pass them by. When writing classified advertisements, you have to concentrate on a good headline and advantages that create an audience response.

When developing property listings, the title is still the main priority, coupled with good advantages, though you must add pictures and colors that the prospects connect to.

When you are writing sales letters or emails, a good outline to follow will be an opening paragraph which draws the reader in and makes them genuinely wish to read more, not toss it in the shredder.

Identify with the prospect regarding the problem they might be dealing with. Relate to them on a psychological level. Reiterate how they think about this, so they see you can connect with them. Talk about the issue, hooking them in. The successful part is going to be the answer you have to this problem.

And that leads to the third component: have a concise and clear call to action. Tell your prospect what you would like them to do. If it is a sales letter, tell them at the end that they have to sign up today for their "free access to X." Whatever you are providing them, give them tips on how to get it. Allow it to be clear and easy for them. If they do not understand where to go or what to do, it spells disaster for your marketing plan.

As you can see, there is a great deal to composing great, solid, successful sales copy. We have only touched on the basics, but this ought to get you started.

Strategy 8
Referrals

The various marketing tools mentioned so far are dependent on the goals. They might share the same goals but will individualize the information they provide.

For instance, you may use the web or newspapers to list properties. Either way, you make an effort to write up distinctive introductions to each property, so customers will not feel as if they're reading through the same text again and again.

These are all paid methods. However, there are marketing methods which you cannot pay for. For instance, the referrals which you receive from other individuals.

If you help someone buy or sell a home, they are going to walk away with memories of that experience. With any luck they'll believe you did everything you could to help them through the process. You can be certain they're going to share any strong feelings about their experience, good or bad. Later on, whenever they meet other people who are buying or selling, they're going to share that story. Therefore, be sure you do all you can to get good ratings by word of mouth.

Here's a fantastic idea for you when you've facilitated a sale. Ask the client to provide you with a video testimonial about how you've helped them get what they need. The video must discuss your services and how they received good results from using you. Put this testimonial on your site for other prospective clients to find.

Doing this will produce far more leads for you than you might imagine. It can easily be hard for customers to choose which real estate agent to pick in an area. When you have clients that have confidence in you, believe in you, and sing your praises, you are going to become the go-to agent in the local market.

Giving out fliers and business cards might seem old fashioned, though they still get interest. They are excellent marketing resources for real estate agents to work with. It can easily be far more relatable if you hand them out at public events and gatherings. Nevertheless, you need to additionally find locations in which you can put them on counters for buyers to see. Try the coffee shop you frequent and the tanning salon you go to, and ask if you can put your business cards on their countertop.

However, the true secret is making certain your marketing material speaks to the consumer. Your material should show the advantages the prospective client will get by using you and only you.

As a REALTOR, it's your duty to make use of all of the effective marketing resources you can, in order to set yourself apart from everybody else.

The Best Real Estate Marketing Plan

Effective marketing techniques are not randomly achieved. Rather, they're the outcome of careful preparation. They're based on proven strategies. A marketing plan covers what is not worth doing too. What remains are lots of options to achieve the results you're after.

Marketing is an element of a thriving real estate business. When users do not have a clue what's readily available for sale, there's no chance they can decide to purchase it. Thus getting the word out there to as many individuals in your target audience as you possibly can is vital. Notice I said audience which means the people who have a specific interest in purchasing real estate. That's a crucial part many people make the error of trying to appeal to too broad a market. They think the greater number of individuals they reach, the greater chance they have of sealing the deal. That is not how it ends up working.

You need to target a certain market. For instance, if you send out information to 10,000 untargeted individuals when only 10 of them are curious after that, you do not have a high conversion rate. What you probably have, however, is a fantastic amount of money spent on marketing that yielded no results. Nevertheless, if you simply target 2,000 specific individuals and you can get 1,500 of them interested after that, you have not invested too much to do it.

There are several simple components to any productive real estate agent marketing campaign. Initially, you need to have all the information gathered about the property for sale. It is inadvisable to promote when important parts are missing. State a cost that will get some offers without overpricing or underpricing. Pictures are important to ensure individuals can see the property.

The above is obviously key to getting interest. However, the majority of the marketing must be innovative. What specifically might help it sell? Could it be the acres of land? The huge backyard with the built-in swimming pool? It may be the location of a premises for the perfect coffee shop or perhaps there's some special story behind the property.

Creating a plan will be your first priority. Consider the industry right this moment and what potential buyers want. When you get a concept, you can start working on the next step! A successful real estate agent understands what the industry is offering in various situations. Before you begin looking for out some customers, you must work out what customers need.

Look into the most popular homes on the marketplace along with the most popular neighborhoods to live in. This is what your buyers wish to learn about. Getting all of this information up front will set you apart from other agents.

Today, you will find loads of marketing aids. Many of these resources are extremely simple to perform and maintain. You will find several simple platforms like newsletters, sites, and email tools to begin with. These are a necessity for every marketing plan. The web is big and new tools are launched every day. Be sure to stay on top of what's available.

You don't have to learn a great deal about the web to start your own website. If you can afford to, consider outsourcing this particular work. You can get a specialist developer without a massive price.

A newsletter will enable you to keep in touch with your clientele. Keep them informed about how the industry is doing and what's happening with the business. Experiment with sending out a few email updates. These emails may be delivered every month to each person on your list.

Never fail to make yourself accessible to the clients too. If they know they can contact you at any time, they're far more apt to sign up with you.

At this time, the market might be hard, but there are plenty of marketing resources for real estate agents today. Marketing can be powerful if you understand how to approach it the proper way. Many businesses have thrived on the Internet and do well promoting themselves and their company online. You'll find a couple of things you must abide by to achieve success on the web.

You need to enhance your bottom line quickly. It is important you know how vital it is to assess every aspect for possible improvements. You likewise have to have a good idea how much you are going to spend on various advertising campaigns. You will find a range of choices to help you boost your Internet visibility. You'll additionally have to have excellent traffic to get noticed by prospects and to convert them to clients.

Once you begin an Internet marketing campaign, you must first access what's necessary. You must determine a market you can target which isn't extremely competitive. Often big companies look for less competitive niches to find new markets which don't involve as much spending on promotion and marketing.

Profitable promotion needs to be competitive and fresh. You need the ability to blow your competition out of the water and establish a clear identity. Occasionally, you can even out-perform huge names for a fraction of the price.

Conclusion

The present real estate market is a tough one. Many people are losing their homes, instead of earning cash from them. This makes it extremely hard for a real estate agent to earn a living. But marketing is an easy task to achieve. To earn in the present situation, you need a solid plan.

You need to take a seat and spend time brainstorming. Write out a list of different ideas and narrow it down to the best one. Also ensure you understand the marketplace in and out. Find out which neighborhoods have the greatest homes at the most effective prices. Assess where the local real estate market is at. It could be extremely tricky to promote a home where the market is too small.

From there, you must begin checking out the marketing tools available, which includes sites, blogs, and newsletters. The web is huge, so use it to get clients through a website or business blogs.

Creating a site is extremely easy. There are many website publishing systems available to do all of the tough work. If you've additional cash to invest, work with a developer to help you get you started. Make sure you add regular updates and provide a newsletter for your clients. This helps to show them you have a real interest in what they require. You can send out updates regarding the newest homes put into the marketplace, along with prices.

Ensure you're constantly obtainable for your clients. By allowing them to know you're available at any time, you'll be easily in a position to pull in additional clients. Be sure to send out emails about news like changes to the law, the economy, or the industry as a whole. The more your consumers understand about the economy, the more likely they are to purchase a new house.

With the information in this primer, hopefully you see real estate marketing does not need to be tough. The real estate market is a challenge, but is on the verge of booming. Today is the time to begin planning your marketing plan. Take the time today to sit and consider which direction you would like to go in.

That way, when you get going, you will have all the customers you desire.